Global Warming and End-Times

A spiritual and scientific issue.

Dr. E. Dean Cook

Global Warming and End-Times
A Spiritual and Scientific Issue.
August 2019

Copyright © Dr. E. Dean Cook, printed in the United States of America. No part of this message can be copied or reproduced without written permission by Wilderness Voice Publishing and the author.

Unless otherwise indicated, all Scripture quotations are from the Holy Bible, English Standard Version ® (ESV®), copyright © 2001 by Crossway, a publishing ministry of Good Publishers. Used by permission. All rights reserved.

Illustrations by Todd Cook

ISBN 978-1-943412-15-0

Published by
Wilderness Voice Publishing
PO Box 857
Canon City, CO 81215
www.mcgmin.com

"A voice crying in the wilderness –
proclaiming the good news of the coming Kingdom!"

TABLE OF CONTENTS

Acknowledgments	5
Introduction	6
One – Is the Earth at Risk?	9
Two – Defining Global Warming	13
Three – Current Views on GW/CC	19
Four – Is GW/CC a Religious Issue?	25
Five – Was Jesus "Green"?	33
Six – Creation Restored	39
Seven – Observations to Guide Us	49
Eight – A Voice from Port Royal and Something to Do	57
Selected Bibliography	63
About the Author	67

ACKNOWLEDGEMENTS

No one can write a book of any significance alone. It is a sincere joy to acknowledge a few special people who helped this writer realize his dream of writing a book on global warming. First, a special thanks to the publisher, Pastor Charles Pretlow, whom I first met when he was a Marine Sergeant and I was his chaplain. I was humbled to have a small part in his coming to faith in Christ and have taken great pride in seeing him develop into a devoted clergyman, writer and publisher. His encouragement to me in writing this book had no small part in its completion.

Secondly, I owe a debt of gratitude to Dr. Sam Gilmore, scientist, professor of biology, avid outdoorsman, seminary graduate and camping companion, for reading the manuscript and offering many helpful suggestions from his rich background of science and experience.

Recognition also goes to my sons, Kevin and Todd, who acted as my editors. Todd also lightened up the subject with his excellent art work. However, the writer takes full responsibility for all errors that might be found.

Finally, Ruth, my dearest companion of 59 years, again acted as my devoted secretary and best critic, honed by her own reading of thousands of books over 70 years.

With all these, I must also acknowledge the leadership of the Spirit of Christ, who I believe inspired and directed the message of this book to all who have ears to hear.

INTRODUCTION

Since childhood, I have been drawn to raw nature. I was born in the rugged Ozarks of central Missouri, so my first and fondest memories are of following my older brother and sister in exploring the environment that surrounded our home. It was our own little Garden of Eden with forests, fields, streams, and a nearby river. We owned a variety of domesticated animals and protected our small chicks from the hawks that sat in the trees above the hen house, hoping for a luscious dinner. Our trees were full of squirrels, our fields full of rabbits, and our river full of fish. Our drinking water came from the wells we had drilled and from a variety of springs that flowed from the hillside. We had all we needed.

When I reached the age of 17, I joined the service and found myself on the Island of Luzon in the Philippines. Here I was immersed in nature again, although of a different kind from what I had known previously. As part of a small contingency of sailors, we were helping to construct a military base on a mountainside overlooking a deep-water bay. Our barracks backed up to a dense jungle filled with all kinds of strange animals and creatures with which I was unacquainted. These strange neighbors consisted of colonies of monkeys, herds of wild boar, many python snakes, and a variety of tropical birds of spectacular colors. We had intruded into their space. When we were not working, we often traveled to a nearby beach to swim and enjoy the sun. This special place provided a rich treasure of tropical fish and barracuda among which we could swim. This was my introduction to another part of creation that existed out of sight and out of mind beneath the sea. My world was expanding and for two years I soaked myself in this natural habitat that will always be a part of my memories.

Following this rare experience, I was sent to another base

A spiritual and scientific issue. 7

north of Seattle, Washington, located on Whidbey Island in the lush Puget Sound. Here creation seemed to exist on a massive scale; the trees, the mountains, the sea and the sky seemed larger than life. As a young airman, I saw this wonderful environment from above, a perspective that only a few were privileged to see. We often took training flights along the coastline, over and through the rugged mountains, and across deserts - a sight that left one breathless.

As time passed, I met and married my wife, Ruth, and we started a family. Now serving as a chaplain, I was assigned to Hawaii and was introduced to this island paradise that God had created from undersea volcanos, which He then populated with beautiful flowers, trees and birds, using the trade winds that blew across the ocean. In contrast to Hawaii's nature, I was later sent to Kodiak Island in Alaska to serve with the Coast Guard and to live among the whales, seals, king crab and the Kodiak bear. We flew all over Alaska, down the Aleutian Chain, and as far north as Barrow on the Arctic Ocean. Later we were sent to Monterey Bay in California, the birthplace of John Steinbeck and the inspiration for not only his writing, but also the works of many other painters, philosophers and poets. Monterey Bay, along with Carmel, Pebble Beach and Big Sur, is one of the most beautiful places on the planet. These unique locations where we were privileged to live, reminded me repeatedly of our creative God who designed this world not only to be our home but also for our enjoyment because He loves us.

Now, in my senior years I am fortunate to live out my days in a log cabin nestled alongside a beautiful gurgling Kentucky stream. As I sit on my front porch and take in the inspiration and peace which surrounds me, I watch squirrels playing tag up and down trees, jumping from limb to limb like acrobats. I hear birds all around me, lifting their songs of praise to God as they enjoy His creation and the mulberry trees that He provides for them. My point is this: I have discovered that I was kind of a naturalist before I knew it was fashionable.

The purpose in writing this small book is to offer the reader a helpful guide through the confusion surrounding global warming. The voices that are being heard today are often loud, fearful and contradictory: "It's apocalypse in twelve years!" "God is in charge and all is well!" "We must stop driving fossil-fueled automobiles!" "I'm proud to drive an SUV!" "When you cut down a tree, you shorten the life of the earth!" "This planet has always existed, and it will continue to do so!" "Endangered species are dropping dead like flies!" "Species have always come and gone!" "We are giving our grandchildren a poisoned planet!" "Technology has always found a solution!"

The coming chapters will examine the cries of alarm voiced today concerning the risk of global warming. We will define global warming and its impact on our planet. We will examine a variety of attitudes on the subject. We will discuss global warming as a religious issue. We will examine Jesus' life and teaching on creation care and look at how He connects global warming to End Times as well as His plan to create a new heaven and new earth. We will present helpful observations and some possible actions we can all take. Chapter 8 introduces Kentucky's renowned naturalist Wendell Berry of Port Royal, who is a major voice in calling for better care of the land and creation. Finally, we present ten myths to disregard in the global warming discussion and ten truths to embrace. We end with three prayers offered for contemplation.

Note: For the sake of brevity, instead of always spelling out "global warming and climate change", the text will often use the form "GW/CC".

CHAPTER ONE
IS THE EARTH AT RISK?

I picked up the May 20, 2019, issue of *Time Magazine* and there it was again: "A million species and human society face dire risk." Who is to blame? The article said human activity was to blame, citing a U.N. biodiversity report that warned of the coming calamity. This report spoke of the loss of species now happening and, in their words, "ten to a hundred times faster" than the average rate over the last ten million years. Such statistics are difficult to verify. However, using this statistic, the loss of species is a major threat to our ecosystems all over the world, according to the writer, Ciara Nugent.

More than 7 billion people on earth, according to Nugent, are exploiting natural resources, causing pollution and driving climate change. It is a major ecological principle that our human activity, threatens marine life, amphibians, insects, and all other animals, in addition to humans, according to the writer. Since our life is linked to all other life, we are all at risk. "We are eroding our very foundations," says Robert Wilson, one of the U. N.'s climate report authors who

Hot and Getting Hotter?

goes on further to say, "We are losing our critical foundations for economics, livelihood, security, health and quality of life."

10 Global Warming and End-Times

These claims are critical but are they really factual? Or, are they inflated by the writer's fears and/or the need to publish? Only God knows!

According to Nugent, scientists are telling us the loss of species and climate change can only be tackled by "transformative" measures such as an overhaul of international trade, massive investment in forests and green energy, and major changes to individual behavior like consuming less meat. While policy makers remain divided on radical changes and investments, Nugent says, "If we can't agree on a plan fast, the future looks bleak for all." Nugent's views are supported by several of the 2020 presidential candidates and other politicians who are telling us we have no more than 12 years to solve this problem.

At the same time, in a more recent *Time Magazine* article the U.N. Secretary General, Antonio Guterres, is pictured on the cover page, standing off the coast of Fiji in water up to his knees. He was visiting Tuvalu which is one of the world's most vulnerable areas to the rising sea. Five years ago, the Fijian government relocated the village of Vunidogoloa to higher ground at a reported cost of half a million dollars. The abandoned village is now under water, due to a rise in sea level that many scientists attribute to GW/CC. Forty more Fijian villages are scheduled to be moved. In response to the rising sea, several small Pacific islands joined together in calling upon the nations of the world to get serious about GW/CC. Some say that the Pacific provides a map or a strategy to navigate the troubled waters all over the world. However, it must be acknowledged that not all leaders in the Pacific region agree with the proposed solutions. The U.N. Secretary-General has placed the full weight of the U. N. into combatting GW/CC. On the other hand, some are telling us to look to Mars or to the Moon where we can develop colonies that could save the precious seeds of the human race should we destroy our earth. The late Cambridge professor Stephen Hawking suggested we

A spiritual and scientific issue. 11

should seriously pursue the colonization of other planets in order to save our own. Our next major space project, which has been announced recently, is to colonize the Moon. The writer recently visited Kennedy Space Center in Florida where this project is well underway.

A Dark Movement

Jonathan Moo and Robert White, in their book *Let Creation Rejoice*, discuss the "Dark Mountain" movement in England led by Paul Kingsnorth. This movement proclaims that there is no longer any hope of our preventing catastrophe and environmental collapse. Moo and White, commenting on this dark movement, write:

> The notion that a so-called perfect storm of factors are coming together in a way that threatens the future of all life on earth, is no longer the unique purview of bearded prophets, street preachers and religious fundamentalists. A United Kingdom chief scientist got a lot of attention when he suggested that we might be witnessing the catastrophic effect of just such a perfect storm as soon as 2030 (p. 13).

The public did not quickly swallow the scientist's 2030-year prediction because some have surmised that we have come to expect that such dire predictions should extend at least 100 years into the future to give us time to respond.

Political Involvement

Since Americans have always been anxious to adopt ideas from Europe, it is possible that many of our alarmists in America today are being influenced by the darker writers of England and Europe. The trend we see in writers and speakers is that they tend to be louder and more radical than in the past. They are forcing the issue of GW/CC upon the public with new fervor. Climate issues have taken on greater significance recently because they are now part of the emotional political debate. For example, a few years ago, Vice-President Al Gore's film and book *An Inconvenient Truth* got major public attention because of his political stature. People assumed he knew things or had seen things only one in his position would have been privileged to know, so they listened and chose to believe him.

Recently, another of our former Vice-Presidents, Joe Biden, while campaigning for the presidential nomination, said that we must adopt a national priority regarding our care of the planet. He then endorsed the Green New Deal, a radical environmental program proposed by a junior congresswoman from New York. Most other candidates in the Democratic Party running for office are also supporting GW/CC plans and projects as part of their platforms. If elected, they foresee these projects having top priority in their administration, not unlike the Manhattan Project did during WWII. It was reported widely in the press that Biden estimated his proposal would cost more than 5 trillion dollars over a ten-year period. This sounds like chicken feed compared to the Green New Deal which is estimated to cost up to 93 trillion dollars over the same period of time. Without additional funding, this cost could absorb the defense fund, the health care fund, transportation fund, education fund, space fund and most of the "funds" in the national budget! Why are so many politicians choosing to use GW/CC as a major part of their campaign? Is it because it draws attention, wins votes, produces jobs and brings financial benefits to industry and big business, or are they more scientific-minded than some? Or have they simply come to realize that people are finally awakening to environmental concerns and they want to capture the wave? Although more people do seem to be listening today, they do not appear to be ready for radical changes in our national priorities or in their personal lives. We are anxious to see where this new awakening will take us.

CHAPTER TWO
DEFINING GLOBAL WARMING

Before we get too far into our subject, we need to define what is meant by "global warming." Simply put, global warming is the slow increase in the temperature of the earth's atmosphere caused in part by greenhouse gases and other factors. These gases are primarily carbon dioxide, chlorofluorocarbons, nitrous oxide, and other pollutants. In other words, earth has a gas problem! The atmosphere has historically provided a kind of escape valve through which these gases could escape the planet. However, scientists tell us that with the increase in our population, industrial production and use of the land, these gases cannot escape through the vents into space. In fact, the gases we are producing in large quantities are forming a blanket over our atmosphere that holds in the heat. This leads to what we call "global warming" which produces "climate change." The Climate Control Independent Organization is made up of leading scientists and journalists who research and report on climate change and its impact on the public. According to this group's statement, first published in their November 2009 newsletter, usually greenhouse gases would be good for the earth; they stabilize the temperature to nearly 33 degrees above what it would be otherwise, making possible life as we know it. The Environmental Protection Agency (EPA) reported that carbon dioxide was to blame for 82% of our greenhouse gases in 2017, followed by methane at 10% (Oh, those cows!) and nitrous citrate at 6%.

Changes are Occurring
The increase in global warming is causing some melting of ice caps and glaciers, creating droughts in some areas, and

14 Global Warming and End-Times

developing catastrophic storms across the world. Those who once lived safely along rivers and streams now find themselves in flood zones. Islands and coastal cities that exist only a few feet above sea level are now threatened by rising waters. Already concerns are being voiced about low coastal U.S. cities such as Miami, New Orleans, and Houston. These climate changes are not only of concern to humans, but they pose a threat to all creatures that inhabit the planet with us. Recently, American farmers lost large numbers of livestock to drowning and fire, while in other areas of the world, animals are starving from lack of food and water. It only stands to reason that this is a special threat to some endangered species.

Okay, who is right?

We must be honest with our history that these tragedies have occurred in the past, and in time we have always recovered or adjusted. But there seems to be something different about today's trends which at the moment are going in the wrong direction. Only God, not man, knows when and if it will end.

Governmental Reporting

The Office of Science and Technology in Washington, D.C., reports that the temperature has risen an average of one-degree F over the last century. Although that does not seem like much, this small change has affected the balance of our climate. According to the EPA, gases of carbon dioxide (CO_2),

A spiritual and scientific issue. 15

methane (CH$_4$), nitrous oxide (N$_2$O), and fluorinated gases are produced as follows:

> **Carbon dioxide** - Carbon dioxide enters the atmosphere through burning fossil fuels (coal, natural gas, and oil), solid waste, trees, volcanos and other biological materials, and also as a result of certain chemical reactions (e.g., manufacture of cement). Carbon dioxide is removed from the atmosphere (or "sequestered") when it is absorbed by plants as part of the biological carbon cycle.
> **Methane** - Methane is emitted during the production and transport of coal, natural gas, and oil. Methane emissions also result from livestock and other agricultural practices and by the decay of organic waste in municipal solid waste landfills.
> **Nitrous oxide** - nitrous oxide is emitted during agricultural and industrial activities, combustion of fossil fuels and solid waste, as well as during treatment of wastewater.
> **Fluorinated Gases** - Hydrofluorocarbons, perfluorocarbons, sulfur hexafluoride, and nitrogen trifluoride are synthetic, powerful greenhouse gases that are emitted from a variety of industrial processes.... These gases are typically emitted in smaller quantities, but because they are potent greenhouse gases, they are sometimes referred to as High Global Warming Potential gases ("High GWP gases"). (Taken from the official EPA website.)

The effect of these gases on global warming depends on three factors: (1) how much is in the atmosphere, (2) how long they stay there, and (3) how powerfully they impact the atmosphere. An important point to be made here is that the Creator originally provided a stable weather system for the earth. It was workable, delicate, efficient and flexible. However, it must be noted that over time the climate did endure periods of instability as evidenced by the research found in the Arctic and other locations. When we began to put stress on the system, it also began to push back. Today this stress seems to be causing measurable consequences.

The rise in the earth's temperature has a clear correlation with our rise in industrialization and population. It is reported that about three-fourths of the world's total carbon dioxide comes from emissions produced by the industrial nations of the U.S., China, India, and Europe. The EPA website reported that in 2017 our total emissions were equal to 6,457 metric tons of carbon dioxide. Sixty percent of that was reported to have come from our use of fossil fuel.

At the urging of the U.N., a climate change conference met in Paris in 2015 to discuss a cooperative effort to slow down, stop, or reverse this rise in temperature. Some 195 countries signed onto the plan known as The Paris Agreement. The goal adopted was to keep the temperature from rising above 1.5-degree C. and to meet every five years to assess the progress. The IPCC (the Intergovernmental Panel on Climate Change), created in 1988 by the World Meteorological Organization to provide governments with climate information to help them craft climate policy, released a report on the difference between warming 1.5 degrees C. and a rise of 2.0 degrees C. The news was not good. At a 2.0 C. increase it was estimated that hundreds of millions of people would be in danger and the planet itself could be damaged.

President Trump's Policy

President Trump, upon taking office in 2017, withdrew our nation's official participation in The Paris Agreement because he said it would require surrendering America's sovereignty to the U.N. on climate decisions. It was suggested that a second reason for his decision was that the U.N. was going to ask the richer industrialized nations to subsidize the poorer ones with their ecological efforts. The President acted

A spiritual and scientific issue. 17

by proposing a committee to study the issue of GW/CC while allowing our scientists to cooperate and participate with the U.N. effort, as unofficial members. Some of the press have painted the President as being hostile to GW/CC. However, others see him as simply being cautious about committing the nation to an open-ended financial obligation. The point is that America is now engaged nationally and internationally in the GW/CC discussion and effort, although many ecologists want the President to do more. Therefore, GW/CC is certain to be a major campaign issue in the coming elections.

The Effect of Increased Population

It is estimated that in Jesus' day there were approximately 3 million people living on the earth. Today it has climbed to nearly 7 billion. Common sense tells us that when a family welcomes the first child, changes must be made. There is less space, more consumption, and more waste. But then, add the second, third, and perhaps the fourth child and potential problems begin to multiply. If adjustments are not made wisely, unforeseen difficulties will occur. This is the picture of where our planet is today. We are a large and growing population of consumers. What the future holds is not totally clear to us, but we must acknowledge that we live in challenging times and a changing environment. Technology may help us but we have no assurance that it can save us. This is not a call for limiting families; however, it is a call to live smarter, simpler and more efficiently, so we can make room for others.

Finally, the human cause of GW/CC is not the settled issue some would have us believe. For example, Dr. Robert Carter, Emeritus Fellow and Science Policy Advisor at the Institute of Public Affairs, and Chief Science Advisor for the International Climate Coalition, writes in the book *Climate Change: The Facts*, "...[H]uman effect on the climate is trivial compared to the natural variations." He refers to such "natural variations" as the radiation of the sun. Dr. Richard Lindzen, Atmospheric Physicist and Professor of Meteorology at M.I.T., states in his essay in the same book, "Climate is pretty insensitive to greenhouse gas." He believes that the impact of greenhouse gas today is being exaggerated.

The writer is well aware that one could list renowned scientists on the other side of the question. So, is the Earth at risk? Perhaps, but on a scale of 1 to 10 no one seems to be able, at this point in time, to give us an accurate number regarding where the Earth's future stands.

CHAPTER THREE
Current Views on GW/CC

It should be noted that global warming and climate change are not the same thing. It is global warming that produces climate change and other effects upon the earth. If one studies the issue of GW/CC, it becomes evident that there are at least four major views on this subject. Let's summarize them for the sake of discussion.

Group One – The Doom and Gloom View

This group might be called the Doom and Gloom Group since they tend to see calamity coming upon us and our planet very soon unless radical change is initiated. The emphasis is on radical change now. Their suggested changes include a major transformation of how we live and relate to the planet. They see solutions as requiring a global effort, with the rich countries subsidizing the efforts of the poorer ones. Specific changes being suggested include ending the use of fossil fuel and making a major shift to reusable energy. It would require a revolutionary change in the design of cars, trucks, planes, buses, trains and power plants. Some have even advocated powering our airplanes with batteries and solar power. A recent international air show featured prototypes of such planes but the technology is far from complete.

It is true that fossil fuel consumption produces lots of greenhouse gases which continue to rise. The word "greenhouse" is a good picture of what is actually happening. When the sun shines through the greenhouse glass it warms the soil and the plants inside that in turn release energy that is unable to escape because of the glass. As a result, the greenhouse temperature rises. In the past we kept a reasonable balance in our earth's greenhouse, but with our increase in gases, our earth is becoming warmer because the pollutants cannot escape. This experience is not unlike the frog in the pot on the hot stove. The water is slowly warming and in time will cook the frog if he doesn't act. This group sees us as the frog who perishes in twelve years.

The Doom and Gloom Group is sincere in their beliefs but their fears and perhaps their lack of faith lead them to call for radical change now.

Several books reflect this view, such as *Collapse of Western Civilization* by Naomi Oreske; *The World Without Us* by Allen Weiseman; *The Uninhabitable Earth* by David Wallace; *The Final Warning* by James Patterson; and *The Water Will Come* by Jeffery Woodell which predicts the rising of the seas and the sinking of coastal cities. These voices tend to be some of the loudest today and are exercising considerable influence over our politics, culture, education and even religion.

Group Two – The Skeptics

This group stands at the opposite end from the Doom and Gloomers. The Skeptics mock the claims of the global warmers and have little interest in radical change. The reasons for the skepticism are many. For example, some people do not respond to a call for radical change because only one in three people believe that GW/CC is affecting their own lives. Others believe that God controls the universe, not man, and thus there is little we can do about it anyway. Yet others do not trust the media's reporting on the subject since they have been known to create or slant stories for public consumption—a problem on both sides of the issue.

The Skeptics have a strong voice in their corner, popular meteorologist Joe Bastardi. He has 40 years of experience studying and forecasting weather and climate change. In his recent book *Climate Chronicles: Inconvenient Revelations You Won't Hear From Al Gore—and Others*, he argues that the Sun, the ocean, other events such as volcanic eruptions, and the

A spiritual and scientific issue. 21

design of our climate system, have far more influence on our climate than do human-made greenhouse gases. He goes on to question the motives of some of the alarmists as perhaps driven by self-esteem, power, control and fortune, more than real concern for the climate. When their past predictions have been wrong, he says, they simply move on and are never held accountable. In addition, he argues that some want to overturn our present economic development model that has served the nation for 150 years. Some may differ with Jo Bastardi, but they cannot refute his 40 years of study and successful forecasting of the weather.

Skeptics also know that some published scientific studies and research have been found to be biased and faulty, casting doubt upon what science reports. Finally, pressure is mounting on the government and the public to take major climate change action now, but the Skeptics believe that we need more study, facts and time before any major changes are initiated.

Group Three – The Conservative Religious View

Although this group can differ significantly in their views of faith and life, a large number of them believe that global warming is first and foremost a religious issue. Their faith in a good, present and reliable God shapes how they think about their lives and determines how they make decisions. Therefore, when voices are raised, blaming religious teaching and people as contributors to global warming, these folks are offended because they believe that their accusers tend to deny God's active presence in creation. They take seriously their duty as stewards of God's creation. While some may fear that their involvement in the GW/CC issue will distract them from their first calling, which is to share the Gospel and save souls, others are coming to understand that the Gospel and creation care are intertwined. It is not wrong to care for souls and whales if we love God and His creation.

On the other hand, many do not believe that God has given people the power or authority to destroy the earth. God will do that Himself when He determines it is time. Neither do they see people as the only cause and solution to the problem. The Scripture says that God created the earth and all that is in it, that He is active in sustaining it and invites us to partner with Him in keeping the planet a viable habitat for us all. However, the Bible is clear that God has, in the past and will again, use climate change as one form of judgement upon our rebellious world that is turning away from Him. This group tends to be more conservative but does not reject the "green" message outright, it's just that they have a strong view based upon Scripture and their faith in the living God.

Group Four – The Bridge-Builders

There is a growing number of people of faith and science who are seeking to build a bridge between various disciplines in finding a solution for GW/CC. This group is presently represented by people such as Dr. Katherine Hayhoe, a professor at Texas Technical University and director of their Climate Change Center. She is also CEO of her own consulting firm on GW/CC. She has published eight books on the subject and written over 125 academic papers reporting on her ecological research. Two of her books are *A Climate of Change* (co-authored with her husband) and *The Climate Report*.

She has participated in numerous GW/CC forums and organizations which include The Global Change Research Program, The National Climate Assessment and The National Academy of Science Report and has given input into "The Climate Stabilization Targets and Emission Concentration Targets for the Decades Ahead." In addition, she has been asked to brief Congress, federal agencies and city administrators. Recently, her research has focused on the impact of GW/CC on human systems and the natural environment that includes studies on its impact on

A spiritual and scientific issue. 23

agricultures, ecosystems, energy, infrastructure, public health and water resources.

Because Dr. Hayhoe is a person of faith and married to an evangelical pastor, she is also given a warm reception by churches and other religious groups. By seeking to bring faith, science, and other disciplines together, she is convincing a growing number of followers that they need to give GW/CC a second look. Her faith and solid scientific research have led her to be a hopeful exponent of bridge-building between religion and science. She avoids a call for radical change but favors smaller changes that are more acceptable to the public because they are less disruptive.

In addition to Dr. Hayhoe, two theologians – Donald Conroy and Rodney Peterson – have edited an excellent book entitled *Earth at Risk*. The book's summary states,

> As a new Millennium dawns, humanity faces the threat of an unmitigated ecological disaster. At first glance, science and religion may seem to be antithetical avenues for solving our many environmental crises. Religion views science as lacking ethical direction, while science regards religion as lacking an empirical foundation for understanding the environment. However, neither science nor religion when viewed separately are adequate to address the serious global threats to earth's ecosystems. In the modern age of globalization, scientific advances, technological growth and trade, an interdisciplinary discussion is needed if all interested partners are to cooperate to resolve problems that affect everyone.

In 1985, a handful of people began to discuss bringing together Christians to assess the ecological crisis of the day. In 1987, they held their first conference at a United Methodist conference ground in Indiana. There they discussed a Christian view of creation care and the crises facing America's small family farms. Before concluding, they gave themselves the name North American Conference on Christian Ecology (NACCE). Since then they have met annually and adopted their mission:

> We will invite people into loving relationship with the earth through the formation of earth-keeping circles. We will teach reverence for God's creation, with the understanding that humans are embedded in the natural world. We will cooperate with other organizations concerned with ecology and social justice. We will promote the study of ecological issues in the context of biblical theology and contemporary science.

The NACCE is an important Christian ecological organization that is reaching out to churches and other faith groups to help them become educated and involved in creation care. Some Christians may not feel comfortable with this group since they do welcome the participation of Muslims, Hindus, Buddhists, and others in the discussion and effort to honor creation. Whatever one's attitude may be, if the Church is to be a public voice on behalf of creation, it must be prepared to stretch itself to help solve the problem that affects us all while keeping true to one's own faith and theology.

In summary, these four major views or attitudes on GW/CC tend to dominate the discussion today. There are countless variations of these four, and even those are in flux. We can say without contradiction that there is not a unanimous opinion on this issue of GW/CC.

CHAPTER FOUR
Is GW/CC a Religious Issue?

As we have noted, science and religion have not always been the closest of friends. A degree of mistrust has characterized their relationship for ages. As science grew in prominence and influence, it replaced the voice of the Church in speaking to issues of creation and its care. The Church, meanwhile, settled into its diminished public role, retiring to pray, ponder theology and care for the faithful. Each now had its own sphere of influence: science was recognized as dominating the material world and the Church dominating the spiritual world, and little dialogue took place between the two. Although the times have changed, remnants of this ancient wall still remain. The Church has been slow to respond to the global-warming issue and the warning of science. At the same time, science is not certain whether the Church's input should be a part of the discussion. However, as the Church becomes

greener, Church leaders are beginning to write and speak on the issue, and are demanding more of a voice at the table. In fact, a number of prominent clergy have been so bold as to state that the issue of GW/CC is first and foremost a religious issue and secondly a scientific one.

Merritt's Movement

Jonathan Merritt, a young conservative clergyperson and the son of a conservative pastor, wrote a book in 2010 that was read widely. It was titled *Green Like God* and was reviewed by *Time Magazine*, which saw it as a significant departure from the Church's conservative

view of GW/CC. *Time's* focus on his book launched Merritt into the center of the Green debate and caused a frenzy in the media. His basic message was so old that it was new again: namely that God had a green thumb, and as Creator had breathed life into dirt and given man the responsibility to care for His creation. Not only was this a "care" issue, but Merritt also held that the Bible taught that God planned to restore creation in the end times and return us to a beautiful planet not unlike the Garden of Eden. He said that our responsibility for creation was a part of God's plan from the very beginning and is a priority for

us today. His book urged the Church and all people of faith to have a seat at the table of GW/CC. In other words, he was saying that no discussion of this issue would be complete without having the input of God and Scripture.

In this chapter and in the one to follow, we will seek to summarize why we agree that GW/CC is primarily a religious issue before it is a scientific or social one.

The Bible and Creation

First, the Bible is the oldest divinely inspired book that addresses creation directly and speaks of our duty to care for it. Other ancient creation accounts exist but their authority and validity are questionable. None of us were present, of course, when God took nothing and in an orderly fashion spoke creation into existence. But we have the account because He

A spiritual and scientific issue.

loved us enough to share it with us. The Scriptures were preserved for us by the Jewish nation and its people, which is a major contribution to creation's history. The record of God's creation is found in the Book of Genesis:

In the beginning God created the heavens and the earth. The earth was without form and void and darkness was over the face of the deep. And the spirit of God was hovering over the face of the waters. And God said, "Let there be light" and there was light. And God saw that the light was good. And God separated the light from the darkness. God called the light Day and the darkness He called Night. And there was evening and there was morning of the first day (Genesis 1:1-2).

Since God is spoken of as Creator, clearly humankind is not, and has never been, the center. Therefore, we must concern ourselves first with His purposes and plan for us and the planet on which He placed us. When we mistakenly place ourselves at the center, we head down a false road that will skew our understanding and response to GW/CC. In the creation order found in Genesis 1:6-26, God made humans last, on the sixth day. Genesis 2:7 says, *"He formed the man of dust from the ground and breathed into his nostrils the breath of life and man became a living creature."* Then in Genesis 2:18-24, we have the creation of Eve from the bone taken from Adam. This tells us that we have a special tie to both the earth and to God.

Our Dominion

The Bible goes on to say that God gave us dominion over the fish of the sea, and over the birds of heaven, and over the livestock, and over all the earth, and over every creeping thing that creeps upon the earth. It says that God also blessed them and said, *"Be fruitful and multiply and fill the earth and subdue it and have dominion over it."* God delegated to Adam and Eve the high calling to keep His creation, but they were to exercise this authority under His direction and supervision. This was a shared effort. In other words, they did not have the freedom to use, abuse, trash, or waste what He had created. They were not only to keep creation as a sacred trust, but they were to improve upon it. The garden in which God placed Adam and Eve may well have been a prototype of His plan for the entire earth, a plan we would play a part in developing.

The Great Fall

In the third chapter of Genesis, the Bible records the sad story of how Adam and Eve listened to their own prideful and doubting hearts as well as the voice of the Dark Angel, Satan. As a result, they turned away from God, their beloved Creator. After their sin, God confronted them; they were full of fear and guilt and tried to hide themselves from Him. Before, they had welcomed His presence and companionship but now everything had changed. This change impacted their relationship to God, to each other, to His lesser creatures and to all the earth itself. Creation was now under a curse and would no longer respond, as it once had, to Adam and Eve. Now broken like us, creation would push back on our efforts, and the lesser creatures of God would come to fear rather than love us. Everything would become harder as suffering, pain, disease and death would invade our once-peaceful world. Despite this unspeakable tragedy, the Bible is clear that God never left us but continued to visit us and struggle to lead us back to the paths of righteousness.

Biblical Laws Governing Creation Care

In God's instructions to His covenant people Israel, He clearly outlines what He expects of them as His children. We read one powerful set of such instructions in Deuteronomy 28:

> *And if you faithfully obey the voice of the LORD your God, being careful to do all his commandments that I command you today, the LORD your God will set you high above all the nations of the earth. And all these blessings shall come upon you and overtake you, if you obey the voice of the LORD your God. Blessed shall you be in the*

A spiritual and scientific issue.

city, and blessed shall you be in the field. Blessed shall be the fruit of your womb and the fruit of your ground and the fruit of your cattle, the increase of your herds and the young of your flock. Blessed shall be your basket and your kneading bowl. Blessed shall you be when you come in, and blessed shall you be when you go out. The LORD will cause your enemies who rise against you to be defeated before you. They shall come out against you one way and flee before you seven ways. The LORD will command the blessing on you in your barns and in all that you undertake. And he will bless you in the land that the LORD your God is giving you. The LORD will establish you as a people holy to himself, as he has sworn to you, if you keep the commandments of the LORD your God and walk in his ways. And all the peoples of the earth shall see that you are called by the name of the LORD, and they shall be afraid of you. And the LORD will make you abound in prosperity, in the fruit of your womb and in the fruit of your livestock and in the fruit of your ground, within the land that the LORD swore to your fathers to give you. The LORD will open to you his good treasury, the heavens, to give the rain to your land in its season and to bless all the work of your hands. And you shall lend to many nations, but you shall not borrow. And the LORD will make you the head and not the tail, and you shall only go up and not down, if you obey the commandments of the LORD your God, which I command you today, being careful to do them, and if you do not turn aside from any of the words that I command you today, to the right hand or to the left, to go after other gods to serve them. But if you will not obey the voice of the LORD your God or be careful to do all his commandments and his statutes that I command you today, then all these curses shall come upon you and overtake you. Cursed shall you be in the city, and cursed shall you be in the field. Cursed shall be your basket and your kneading bowl. Cursed shall be the fruit of your womb and the fruit of your ground, the increase of your herds and the young of your flock. Cursed shall you be when you come in, and cursed shall you be when you go out. The LORD will send on you curses, confusion, and frustration in all that you undertake to do, until you are destroyed and perish quickly on account of the evil of your deeds, because you have forsaken me. The LORD will make the pestilence stick to you until he has consumed you off the land that you are entering to take possession of it. The LORD will strike you *with wasting disease and with fever, inflammation and fiery heat, and with drought and with blight and with mildew. They shall pursue you until you perish. And the heavens over your head shall be bronze, and the earth under you shall be iron. The LORD will make the rain of your land powder. From heaven dust shall come down on you until you are destroyed* (Deuteronomy 28:1-24).

This was an amazing statement addressed to His people Israel, but few today have ever heard these words. In this passage God connects our obedience to Him directly with how the earth responds to us. In other words, God has designed our creation care so that it is a spiritual exercise. We bring blessings or curses upon ourselves, depending upon how we live before Him. Would that all people concerned with the creation today could understand and incorporate this basic truth into their lives.

Fourteen Ecological Laws

In addition to the passage above, there are fourteen distinct laws in the Pentateuch (first five books of the Bible) that address our treatment and care of animals, birds, trees, crops, the land, etc. These can be found in the books of Exodus (chapter 23), Leviticus (chapter 25), and Deuteronomy (chapter 14). To neglect our duty to creation is, according to the Bible, a grievous sin committed against God for which we will be held responsible. The Scripture is also careful to warn us not to overdo it and turn to worshiping the creation rather than the Creator. This warning is written into the first of the Ten Commandments provided to Moses upon Mt. Sinai and is repeated throughout Holy Scripture.

Additional Ecological Bible References

The entire Old Testament consistently speaks of creation care as a religious issue. For example, in Genesis chapter nine, He makes a covenant with Noah, the animals, and the Earth, establishing it with the sign of the rainbow. The songs from Israel's songbook (Psalms) are full of acknowledgement that the earth not only belongs to God but our care of it is our sacred

A spiritual and scientific issue. 31

duty. The Book of Leviticus reveals that the priests were to play a major role in caring for creation also. The prophets were also unified in their message that there was a vital connection between our obedience to God and creation's response to us. For example, Isaiah the prophet wrote, *"The earth lies defiled under its inhabitants; for they have transgressed the laws, violated the statutes, broken the everlasting covenant. Therefore, a curse devours the earth and its inhabitants suffer from their guilt"* (Isaiah 24:5-6).

Therefore, the Bible is the first and most indispensable source of instruction in our understanding of our relationship to GW/CC. Next we will explore the New Testament and Jesus' teaching on this subject.

CHAPTER FIVE
WAS JESUS "GREEN"?

The New Testament's Gospel of John says, *"In the beginning was the Word, and the Word was with God, and the Word was God. All things were made through Him and without Him was not anything made that was made. In Him was life and the life was the light of men"* (John 1:1-5). This passage reminds us that Jesus was not only God's Son, but He was actually God Himself. The book of Colossians, chapter one, supports this by saying that He created all things in Heaven and Earth. So, to use a modern concept, if God is "green", Jesus is "green," also, for they are One.

The Incarnation and Creation

If we were to try to identify the greatest single act of God to prove that He loves us and all creation, we would have to point to the incarnation of Christ, which was Christ clothing Himself in human flesh. The fact that He freely chose to leave His throne in Heaven and come to earth to be born into and live in creation with us is an astounding and mind-boggling fact. Many philosophers and religious leaders of the past considered the incarnation as "below God" and incomprehensible.

John 1:1-5

Politicians, during election years, often leave their comfortable surroundings and visit the depressed Appalachian areas in our Eastern Kentucky where they observe, take photos, talk with, and sympathize with the people who live there. Then they climb back into their helicopters or large SUV's and speed back to their own comfortable surroundings. Their stay in Appalachia is usually only a few hours or a day or two at the most and they are gone. No wonder the mountain people have become skeptical of politicians who profess concerns for them and their poverty during election years.

If the traditional site of Jesus' birth at Bethlehem is correct, His incarnation actually happened below the earth in a cave used as a crude cattle stall. One cannot arrive at a lower point than that. Unlike some of our politicians who visit brokenness for only a few hours and then leave, Jesus chose to live His entire life with us. Therefore, the incarnation of Jesus stands as God's epic statement of His love for us and the conditions under which we struggle.

Jesus and Creation Care

If fully recorded, the report of what Jesus both said and did to teach us about the care of creation would, I suppose, fill many shelves in the world's libraries. For the sake of this brief work, we have chosen only a few of His most profound teachings and examples of the value and care of creation:

"Do not waste": Matthew 14:13-21 – In this passage Jesus demonstrates His desire that we waste not the Earth's resources. On this occasion Jesus performs a miracle by feeding more than 5,000 people who had come out to hear Him share the Bread of the Gospel. Following His teaching, He performed a miracle and fed the multitudes who had missed their meal. All were given what they needed and were satisfied, after which Jesus' disciples (no doubt under His instructions) gathered up 12 baskets of leftovers so that none would be wasted. This is an amazing detail that after a long and exhausting day He should notice and care for the leftovers. I have always wondered what Jesus did with those leftovers. Did He share them with the

A spiritual and scientific issue.

poor? Did He distribute them among strangers? Or did He share them with the animals and birds which God is also responsible for feeding? The point is that Jesus took the time to teach His disciples not to waste the earth's resources. Is that not a powerful lesson for today's culture?

"Authority over storms": Luke 8:22-25—In this passage Jesus is crossing the Sea of Galilee with His disciples when He falls asleep from exhaustion. While He sleeps the boat encounters a fierce windstorm that seems to threaten its passengers with sinking. The disciples, in a panic, awaken Jesus and scold Him for sleeping during the crisis. The Bible says that Jesus responded by rebuking the wind and the raging waves whereby they became calm again. Then He rebuked the disciples by asking them why they did not have faith. They respond by asking each other, "Who is this that He commands the wind and water and they obey Him?" Like so many of us, they had their own questions but never got around to answering His!

This event is filled with rich teaching material about our own response to creation's storms. Notice that Jesus, who placed Himself into creation, still has the authority to control it. His rebuke of the disciples seems to imply that if they had faith in Him, they might also be able to do something about storms. It raises the question about our fears when threatened by our environment. Do we have faith that God will care for us and help us with the crisis, or must we rely only on ourselves? This is a significant question that is often avoided by environmentalists who are tempted to leave God out of the picture today.

"Healing properties of creation": John 9:1-7 – Here we are given an interesting account of Jesus healing a man's blindness by mixing His spittle with dirt to make mud, and then placing it upon the man's eyes as a healing compress. The blind man receives his sight to the amazement of all. What is Jesus teaching us by His use of material from the Earth, mixing it with His divine power, to bring healing to the human body?

This event seems to open the door to the idea of the value of earth's properties as a healing agent for the body.

"Our accountability": Matthew 25:14-29 – In this account Jesus tells the story of a man who left his property in the keeping of his servants and took a long journey. When he returned, he called each servant to himself and asked that they give an account of their dominion over his property. Some of the servants had been obedient and had not only kept the property but increased its value. However, one is rebuked harshly because he kept the property but failed to increase its value. The message here is interesting in that it teaches us that as good stewards of God's creation we have the responsibility to not only keep creation but also to make it better. We must confess that too often we fail Him at this point and feel no guilt.

"Palm Sunday and creation": Mark 11:1-9 – Finally, Jesus' procession into Jerusalem on Palm Sunday is ripe with lessons about how Jesus saw creation and His relationship to it. For example, He asks for a young colt to be brought to Him for His ride into the city. The text tells us that this was a colt on which no one had ever ridden. This meant the animal was untried and unfamiliar with its duties to a rider. But when Jesus mounts the untried colt it submits to His touch and His weight, obeying Him thoroughly. This is a powerful statement on Christ's authority over the creatures He had made. Secondly, when the crowd that came out to greet Him begins to shout and sing praises to Him, the Pharisees seek to quiet them. Jesus responds by saying that if He quieted the crowd, then the rocks themselves would cry out. This is an intriguing statement about Jesus' relationship to His creation, which in this case were inanimate objects. Notice how even the rocks, which have no tongue, desire to praise and worship Him. Finally, the account says that the people in the processional wave palm branches cut from trees to celebrate His triumphal entry into Jerusalem. They

A spiritual and scientific issue. 37

used these items taken from creation to honor Him as King and Jesus fully accepted these elements of worship.

Was Jesus "green"? The answer can only be, "Yes!" He even took the bulk of His teaching about His Kingdom directly from nature by talking about sheep, wheat, water, trees, vineyards, seeds and sparrows. Jesus' life on earth was immersed in nature - seeing it, enjoying it, correcting it, using it, advancing it, and exercising authority over it. Even His choice of death speaks of His relationship to the Earth. He chose to die on a "tree" and awaited His resurrection in a stone sepulcher carved from the earth.

CHAPTER SIX
CREATION RESTORED

Up to this point we have examined the Lord who, as Creator, came and lived among us in His creation. Now, however, near the end of His ministry Jesus takes us to a whole new level in our understanding of creation: He announced that life on earth as we know it will someday come to an end. According to Jesus we should be preparing for end times that will usher in a new Heaven and a new Earth. This is monumental news the world needs to hear. Media, science and culture are generally ignorant of this major teaching. So, why is this end times teaching so important for us to understand? Because this teaching not only outlines God's plan for the future of our earth and its inhabitants, it also reveals the limitations humans have over the future of the earth. It also addresses the "signs of the times" to give us forewarning of when the end is near. Let's look closer at some of these teachings.

Tribulations Leading to End Times

Although there are many veiled references to end times in the Old Testament, Jesus laid the issue fully on the table in Matthew 24 and 25 when His disciples asked Him about certain major changes that He had said would take place in the future. Matthew 24:7ff records how Jesus told His disciples that in the last days *"[N]ation will rise against nation, kingdom against kingdom, and there will be famine and earthquakes in various places. All this is but the beginning of birth pains."* He then referenced the prophet Daniel and adds in verse 21-22, *"For then will be great tribulation such as has not been since the beginning of the world until now, no, and never will be. If those days had not been cut short, no human being would be saved. But for the sake of the elect, those days will be cut short."*

So, what is it that triggers God's decision to end life on earth as we know it? Only one thing: it is the degree of our sinful rebellion against Him.

Jesus, speaking of the last days in Matthew 24:11-12, said, *"And many false prophets will arise and lead many astray. And because lawlessness will be increased, the love of many will grow cold."* In verses 38-39 He adds, *"For as in those days before the flood, they were eating and drinking, marrying and giving in marriage until the day when Noah entered the Ark, and they were unaware until the flood came and swept them all away, so will be the coming of the Son of Man."* In other words, they were so engrossed in their life and in their pleasures and sins that they failed to listen to the message God had delivered to them through Noah. They were apparently blind to the symbolism and message of the Ark that was under construction publicly. So, the Bible says the flood did come as promised and it swept them all away. Because they had no place for God in their lives, He had no place for them on the Ark. Genesis 6 says of the days of Noah:

> *The LORD saw that the wickedness of man was great in the earth, and that every intention of the thoughts of his heart was only evil continually. And the LORD regretted that he had made man on the earth, and it grieved him to his heart. So the LORD said, "I will blot out man whom I have created from the face of the land, man and animals and creeping things and birds of the heavens, for I am sorry that I have made them* (Genesis 6:5-7).

Conditions had become so bad, and the destruction so deep and wide, that to leave things as they were was not an option for God or His creation. The description of the days prior to the flood is in many ways a mirror image of our own culture today - culture that has turned its back on God.

The Influence of Sin

Society at large as well as many in the Church (sad to say) have rejected the written account of Noah and the Flood by

A spiritual and scientific issue. 41

considering it a myth, along with the sin that brought on this tragedy. The biblical Tribulation that will precede the end of the Earth as we know it is also a period of grace given by God, calling us to repent from sin. What is "sin"? Sin is our willful choice to disobey our Creator. Sin rejects God's rule over us and seeks to usurp His authority. We will discover later in our study of Jesus' Book of the Revelation, that this attitude and spirit will become incarnate in a powerful world leader, who will call all people to follow him in his rebellion against God and people of faith. In the Church he is referred to as the Anti-Christ, or the false Christ, who will persecute Christ's followers in the End Times. Instead of prevailing in his wicked plan, he will bring down God's judgement upon himself, his followers and the world. But God will protect a remnant that is faithful to Him.

This is why the faithful must be given a place in the discussion of the End Time crisis. Although, as in the days of Noah, many today are not prepared to listen to the voice of people of faith, God still demands that the truth be told. The tribulation period will witness powerful signs that the end is fast approaching. Daniel the prophet, whom Jesus quoted, describes this as a time of chaos and turmoil lasting seven years. Whether the number seven is literal or spiritual, we cannot say, but it does seem to indicate that it is a relatively short period of time. In Revelation chapters five through nineteen, we are exposed to a crumbling world order so shocking and so full of suffering that it pains us even to read it or to think about it. This is why most of the Church, and much of the godless culture today, ignores its warnings and chooses to go blindly on as they did in the days of Noah. The scroll that contains the full account of end times is pictured in the Revelation as firmly in God's right hand and no one is found worthy to take the book, break the seals and open it. That is, no one but Christ, the Lamb of God. (Revelation 5:1-9)

The Breaking of the Seals

Jesus takes the scroll from the right hand of God and begins to open the seven seals. The scroll reveals, among other things, the four horses and their riders of the Apocalypse. These four horses, all of different colors – white, red, black and pale, symbolize the destruction that will soon be visited upon the earth in quick succession. (Revelation 6:1-8)

The Bible says great earthquakes and darkness will cover the earth, the stars will fall from the heavens, while the mountains and islands will be moved out of their places. One would imagine that all those experiencing this suffering would be full of fear and would immediately respond by repenting of their sins. However, we read that they refuse to repent of their wrong-doing and, like Adam and Eve, try to hide themselves from God's presence. How preposterous!

The Blowing of Seven Trumpets

Next, in chapter eight seven angels are pictured blowing seven trumpets. These seven trumpets announce seven more judgements, all more intense than the seven horsemen. One-third of the earth will be burned up and one-third of the sea will be polluted, along with the rivers and springs. In addition, one-third of the daylight hours will be given to darkness and in the middle of these, great swarms of locust-like creatures will pour forth from a hole in the earth to sting people like scorpions, causing even greater suffering. Finally, a wicked and cruel army that has been kept at the Euphrates River is released against the people, resulting in one-third of all people dying. The reason for this invasion and the cruel carnage that follows is not known but we can assume that the victims were people who refused to obey the Evil One.

Again, one would certainly expect that anyone seeing or experiencing such awful devastation would immediately cry out for mercy and seek the face of God. Instead, Revelation 9:20 tells us that those not killed by the plagues still did not

A spiritual and scientific issue.

repent of the works of their hands, nor cease to worship demons and gods of gold, silver, bronze, stone, and wood. They show no desire to abandon their wicked lives and join God in caring for creation. The real battle they face is spiritual. Part of the Tribulation is going to be global warming, climate change, earthquakes, and other phenomena which we have yet to experience in such magnitude and intensity.

The Power of Two Witnesses

In chapter eleven we are shown the depths of the world's rebellion against the Creator and the hardness of their hearts against Him. In this occurrence God sends two righteous witnesses into the streets of Jerusalem with a word for the people. However, the people refuse to hear the word and respond by killing the two witnesses, leaving their bodies to be desecrated in the streets. Meanwhile the crowd breaks forth in celebration over having eliminated the two witnesses sent to save them. They celebrate as if it were Christmas – there is the feasting and the sending of gifts. They are shocked, however, when God, after three days, raises the two witnesses to life before the eyes of their tormentors. God then takes the two witnesses up into Heaven. The people are stunned and full of fear, but they still do not embrace God or repent of their wicked ways. This occasion reminds us again of the hardness of the human heart when it is set against God.

Twenty-Four Elders

In Revelation 11:15ff we have the blowing of the seventh trumpet which sets in motion the 24 Elders seated on their thrones before God, falling on their faces in worship. The elders then utter these profound words; *"The time has come for judging the dead, for rewarding your servants the prophets and your saints and those who reverence your name ... <u>and for destroying those who destroy the earth.</u>* [emphasis added]." Remember these words for they are key to the subject under discussion. This is a preview of what is soon to happen when God's judgements are complete. <u>The destroyers of the earth will be destroyed</u>. One cannot make a stronger case than this for arguing that the future of the earth is a spiritual issue before it is a scientific one.

The Mighty Warrior

Chapter 19 introduces us to a mighty warrior who is mounted on a white horse. He is called "faithful and true." Written on His robe and thigh are the words "King of kings and Lord of lords." He is ready for battle and His enemies quickly attack Him. He responds by slaying them all, not with a sword of iron but by the sword of God's Word. Most of the world, and perhaps many in the Church, have yet to understand the power of God's Word to defeat evil. This mighty warrior then captures the Beast and the False Prophet who had deceived the people on Earth. He casts them both into the lake of fire. This is part of His plan to destroy the destroyers of His creation. In addition, the Devil, the Father of All Lies, is also captured and cast into the lake of fire along with his evil companions.

Coming of the New Heaven and New Earth

John then says, *"I saw a new heaven and a new earth for the first heaven and the first earth had passed away"* (Rev. 21:1). Earlier in 20:11, he made a similar statement by saying, *"I saw a great white throne and him who was seated on it. From his presence earth and sky fled away and no room was found for them."* Since our book is primarily focused on GW/CC and End Times, we will limit our discussion of the new Heaven and New earth, leaving that for other writers. It is important, however, to point out that Revelation chapters 21 and 22 are full of ecological imagery describing the new Heaven and new Earth. First, the curse placed upon the earth after Adam and Eve sinned will be lifted. All creation now will be free to respond to God and His people. Earth's people and creatures will live in a world free from all fears and threats. Death will be no more, and

A spiritual and scientific issue.   45

suffering and pain will fly away. Our new surroundings will provide all our needs in abundance and more! The trees will be for the healing of the people and the river, clear as crystal, flowing from God's throne, will quench every thirst and water the earth. No night shall darken the sky, for God and Christ will be its light and the Tree of Life will be available for all forever. Our climate will then be perfect.

Isaiah saw this wonderful new Heaven and Earth and recorded his vision in Isaiah 11:6-9. This vision given him from God focuses on the harmony that will be enjoyed between God, His people and all His creatures in the new Earth:

> *The wolf shall dwell with the lamb, the leopard shall lie down with the young goat, the calf and the lion and the fatted calf together and a little child shall lead them, the cow and the bear shall graze, their young shall lie down together; and the lion shall eat straw like the ox. The nursing child shall play on the hole of the cobra, the weaned child shall put his hand on the adder's den. They shall not hurt nor destroy in all my holy mountain for the earth shall be full of the knowledge of the Lord as the waters cover the sea.*

Isaiah 11:6-9 Describes things to come!

This splendid description of God and all His creatures living together in the new Earth in harmony is unsurpassed in all literature. This passage also stands against all accusations that religious people and their teachings are guilty of harming rather than loving creation.

John Muir

John Muir (1838-1910) was America's greatest naturalist. After experiencing an accident which blinded him in one eye for months, his life was changed. Upon receiving his sight again, he vowed to use his new sight to look only upon nature, and that is about all he did for the rest of his life. Muir became the father of America's national park system, wrote ten books on the wilderness and hundreds of articles for magazines and newspapers. However, Muir blamed Christianity for much of the trashing of creation. For example, while walking near Yosemite one day he came upon a large bear which had apparently died of natural causes. But Muir used this encounter with the dead bear to denounce Christianity by arguing that it had allowed no room in Heaven for this noble creature. His argument was part of his belief that Christianity taught that only people were of value to God and thus they could waste the rest of creation. An unworthy accusation of God's people.

Although we respect Muir as a devoted naturalist and confess that our country owes him a great debt for awakening us to the enormous treasures God has given us in nature, he was not without his own flaws. By focusing primarily on nature, he failed to hear God's Word regarding that creation. Had he done so he would have discovered that God had taught His people the value of nature long before Muir ever walked the Sierra Nevada. Over time, Muir became so obsessed with nature that he saw it as nearly synonymous with God, believing that wild nature had greater value than culture or civilization.

Christianity is not perfect and has made many mistakes in its history, but being the archenemy of creation is not one of

A spiritual and scientific issue.

them. For example, John Wesley, the father of Methodism, gave much thought to the suffering of animals. In his sermon "The General Deliverance," written in 1782 and based upon Romans 8:19-22, he states:

> If the creator and father of every living thing is rich in mercy toward all; if he does not overlook or despise any of the work of his own hands, if he desires even the meanest of them to be happy according to their degree—how comes it to pass that such complication of evils oppresses, yea, overwhelms them?

Wesley goes on to answer his own questions by stating that all animal suffering is the result of the Fall. Animals before the Fall were at peace with humanity and with one another, he said, but when sin entered the world, they became predators, waging war against one another. Wesley believed that one day, in the new Earth, God would restore creation to a state more wonderful than ever before. He concluded that no rage or thirst for blood would be found in any creature in the new Earth. It is true that from time to time individual Christians have behaved badly toward God's creation and its creatures and for this we are truly sorry. Still, it should always be remembered that God never advocated or excused such behavior.

CHAPTER SEVEN
OBSERVATIONS TO GUIDE US

Finally, let us make some critical observations that have emerged from our study that would seem to connect GW/CC with End Times.

Observation No. 1
First, we need to find our way out of the ecological confusion surrounding GW/CC. We must acknowledge that it is a religious issue and that little progress can be made until people acknowledge this fact. God, not humanity, is the Creator and center of this universe. Therefore, we have not been given the capacity to destroy the earth, as some today claim. It will be destroyed but by God and at such time as He determines.

Observation No. 2
Humankind was delegated the task of having dominion over, caring for, and subduing creation under God's divine direction. Our failure to fulfill this role has damaged our relationship to Him, to ourselves, to others and to the created order. The Bible, which has been divinely revealed and preserved for us, is our inspired guidebook on how we are to relate to God and serve Him in our dominion role.

Observation No. 3
Our sinful behavior has damaged creation. The heart of people (that is, their willfulness) must be dealt with as part of the GW/CC issue. Patriarch Bartholomew, former head of the Greek Orthodox Church in Constantinople, was a strong proponent of the theology of creation. In his 1997 address in Santa Barbara, California, he stated:

> To commit a crime against the natural world is a sin and for human beings to cause a species to become extinct and to destroy

the biological diversity of God's creation, for human beings to degrade the integrity of the earth by causing it to change its climate, by stripping the earth of its natural forest or by destroying the wetlands, for human beings to destroy other humans with disease by contaminating the earth, water, its land, its air, and its life with poisonous substance – all of these are sins.

This is one of the strongest statements to come from the religious community regarding our relationship to the earth. In 2002 the same patriarch met with Pope Paul II and they signed a declaration which said:

What is required is an act of repentance on our part and a renewed attempt to view ourselves, one another, and the world around us within the perspective of the divine design for creation. The problem is not simply economic and technological; it is moral and spiritual. A solution at the economic and technological level can be found only if we undergo, in the most radical way, an inner change of heart, which can lead to a change in lifestyle of unsustainable patterns of consumption and production. A genuine conversion in Christ will enable us to change the way we think and act.

These two voices, one Roman Catholic and the other Greek Orthodox, joined with a large number of Protestant leaders in speaking with one voice on this matter. God, humankind, sin and our conversion through Christ are key elements in understanding our creation crisis and turning us from our destructive ways. Perhaps a proper beginning would be for the churches to join together to lead the world's inhabitants in a period of confession and renewal of faith in the Creator.

Observation No. 4

Given Observation No. 3, we can further assert that ecological care cannot be forced on people but is a matter of our free will. Even Jesus said that many on the Earth would not choose to repent or change their behavior. This will ensure that climate change will definitely be a part of our future. So,

A spiritual and scientific issue.   51

how does this connect to End Times? We make a major mistake when we put all the blame for global warming on our production of greenhouse gases. It is clear in the Bible that our failure to be obedient to God and good keepers of our planet will, in the end, invite His ecological judgement upon us. James Nash, in his book *Loving Nature*, says, "Christians can't perceive God as exercising ecological judgement against ecological sins." How quickly we forget the days of Noah and the judgements listed in the Book of Revelation.

Observation No. 5

Yet another observation is that we are all linked together, so that what happens to one affects us all. In my experience serving aboard ships at sea, I saw this powerful metaphor demonstrated time and again. When people assigned to the ship chose bad behavior, they put the whole ship and its crew at risk. For example, on one occasion a crew member terrorized the ship by setting fires at night. Another threw over the side of the ship valuable tools and equipment that were needed for its mission. In another instance, a crew member was caught trying to sabotage the ship's engines by putting foreign objects in the gears. The most repugnant was a crewman who defecated in key spaces all over the ship where fellow crew members would encounter the evidence of his disgusting behavior. When these kinds of negative actions occurred in our small community, our ship's crew gave the highest priority to searching out the culprits and stopping their hostile acts.

Recently, while walking in a city park, I came upon a dead crayfish in the middle of the asphalt path. There was a small stream that ran through the park, but this poor crayfish was a long way from the stream. As I considered his dilemma, it occurred to me what had happened. Someone had taken the crayfish from the stream, carried it so far away that it could never get back and left it to die on the hot pavement. Since it was only a crayfish, it might seem like a small thing, but the more I thought about it the more I saw it as a cruel act. The person who did it probably never considered that he or she and that crayfish were linked together as residents on the same small ship sailing through space. And yet by harming that fragile creature, I believe they harmed themselves and us all in ways we do not understand.

In his book *God is Green*, Jonathan Merritt mentions a famous Bible teacher and theological seminary president who contributed to the training of pastors through his writings. This highly respected clergyman reveals his lack of sensitivity to our place in God's creation. Merritt quotes him as writing in a prestigious commentary:

> In God's law neither man nor nation can hold title to either land nor sea and let them remain undeveloped.... The ignorant savage cannot hold large territories of fertile land merely for a hunting ground. When the developer comes he must retire.... Mere priority of occupancy on a given territory cannot be a barrier to the progress of civilization. Wealth has no right to buy a county or state or a continent and turn it into a park. The Earth is man's.

This religious leader who lived from 1843 to 1914 was a product of his day in which exploitation was accepted as a necessity for civilization's progress. However, we must understand that there are many leaders today who hold to this flawed philosophy which says we have the right to pillage the earth under the guise of human progress.

On the other hand, we have some who want to exalt nature to a position next to God. John Muir, the great American naturalist mentioned earlier, came close to this view. He related to components of nature as almost literal brothers and sisters. He even implied on one occasion that he could talk with the rocks, although it is hard to know if he meant this literally or spiritually. St. Francis of Assisi, who is famous for his close relationship to nature, also called birds and animals his brothers and sisters. He

A spiritual and scientific issue. 53

also wrote a hymn titled, "All Creatures of Our God and King" which comes close to extolling nature as a god. However, St. Francis did not place nature above God but was careful to celebrate God's presence in His creatures. This is a significant difference. Among the stanzas he wrote are these words: "All creatures of our God and King, lift up your voice and with us sing." He continues, "Thou rushing wind that art so strong, ye clouds that sail in heaven along." His last verse goes, "Let all things their creation bless and worship Him in humbleness; O praise Him, Alleluia, Alleluia! Praise, praise the Father, praise the Son and praise the Spirit, three in one." Some might say that St. Francis went too far, but others would argue that "we" don't go far enough.

Observation No. 6

Let us conclude with this final observation: if we are going to be honest keepers of creation, we must care for the least of God's creatures among us. This means that we must care for the poor who suffer first and longer from the changes in climate and damages to creation. We must care for the unborn in the mother's womb, who have no voice and often no defenders. We must care for the elderly, the sick, the broken, the outcasts, the lost and the imprisoned. To claim that we are devoted to creation care while ignoring or trashing these vulnerable people is the height of hypocrisy. We must not only care for the least among us, but we must also make room for them in the inn, even if it means our having to move over! This is the true expression of God's love in our hearts and behaviors.

Toward a Theology of Creation Care

Finally, the writer searched for a fitting metaphor or model to help us put the pieces of this complex puzzle together in order to form a clear image of our subject. As I was sitting in worship recently, the scripture lesson for that Sunday was read from Genesis, chapter forty-one. I had read it many times before and was familiar with its message but at that moment the Spirit seemed to illuminate it as the metaphor and model for which I had been searching. So here it is:

In Genesis 41, verses 1ff, it says the Pharaoh of Egypt dreamed that he was standing by the Nile and saw seven well-fed cows come up out of the River. These cows were attractive and healthy, but they were followed by seven emaciated cows, and yet the poor cows consumed the fat cows. He then dreamed a second dream in which he saw seven ears of grain, good and full, but then he saw seven other ears of grain that were thin and damaged by the wind. In the dream the bad ears swallowed the good ears. Pharaoh awoke troubled from these dreams but could find no wise men to interpret them. When an aide informed him that there was a Hebrew named Joseph who could interpret dreams, Pharaoh sent for him.

Joseph, filled with God's spirit, told Pharaoh that the dreams were from God and that God was revealing to Pharaoh that there were to be seven years of good harvest followed by seven years of famine. In short, serious climate change was coming to Egypt and the surrounding area. Joseph also told Pharaoh that this famine was fixed by God; that is, no one could change it and it was to come shortly. The young interpreter told Pharaoh that he was to gather and save the grain and resources the first seven years so that Egypt could survive the last seven. Pharaoh listened intently to Joseph and made the decision of his life: because he saw that the spirit of the Lord was in this young man, Pharaoh placed Joseph in a position over Egypt, second only to himself, to manage Pharaoh's response to this climate change. Joseph was only 30 years of age when he received this high appointment.

This account is a treasure trove of truth for all who would seek to understand GW/CC, and creation care. First, we are reminded that God knows the future and He is thinking about it. He knows our understanding is limited and we need His divine help and guidance. Like Pharaoh, we need to hear and

A spiritual and scientific issue.

to respond to God's word and follow His plan in detail. We need leadership that is responsive to spirituality so they might properly guide us in times of crisis. With God's help, Joseph was able to manage those 14 years of climate change and save Egypt's people, along with many others in surrounding nations. After the crisis was past, we discover from this story that God had an even greater plan for the use of these 14 years of climate change. This was to help mold Joseph's family into a nation and a kingdom of priests who were called to serve God's purpose in the world. This purpose included their receiving a true form of worship, the Ten Commandments, a call to demonstrate His holiness to the world, and to bring forth its Savior. These profound facts have been recorded in sacred Scripture for thousands of years and stand today as a granite monument reminding us that the great issues of life are all spiritual. Since this is true, then GW/CC carries a profound message for us and may well be our first great sign that end times are approaching.

CHAPTER EIGHT
A VOICE FROM PORT ROYAL AND SOMETHING TO DO

As we prepare to conclude our study, it is fitting that we should mention Kentucky's most famous naturalist/poet/author/farmer and avid spokesman for our relationship to creation and the land. I refer to Mr. Wendell Berry of Port Royal, Kentucky, where he lives a simple lifestyle on a humble farm yet is a respected voice among "environmentalists" today (a designation he does not prefer). In his book *The Gift of Good Land*, he shares his deep conviction about being a responsible citizen of the planet:

> To live we must break the body and shed the blood of creation. When we do this knowingly, lovingly, skillfully and reverently, it is a sacrament. When we do it ignorantly, greedily, and destructively, we condemn ourselves to spiritual and moral loneliness and others to want. (p. 129)

Berry clearly sees our care of creation as an act of spirituality. He also believes that there is urgency about all this since he sees the consequences of our past behavior now coming home to roost. At the same time, he is hopeful and believes that no matter how bad it gets we can always improve on things. His appeal to us is to live together in unity and treat the earth with sanctity and love. His fear is that if we fail to do so, we will perish together. Berry's weakness is that he offers no answer as to how we should motivate people to make the needed change.

He believes that the answer to GW/CC will not come by doing one or two big things but by our doing many small things together. Berry is an active member of his church and participates in a number of church-sponsored creation-care projects. As a person who lives what he preaches, he is a sought-after speaker who represents a common sense approach in a day of alarmists. For example, he is a strong advocate for small farms over industrialized agriculture which he sees as often failing to respect the purpose and nature of the land. Besides providing land for his crops, he believes in leaving plenty of woodlands and meadows for balance. His speeches, writings and poetry are read widely and are very influential throughout our state.

As we have been warned before, Berry confirms that climate change is affecting us today, because we continue to assume that it is our right to do what we want with God's creation. If we were able to start changing GW/CC now, the results would still not be seen tomorrow. Turning the weather around is like turning a large ship around at sea. Changing course will be a slow process that can only happen over a long period of time. Since behavior patterns do not change quickly, the challenge is this: are people motivated enough and patient enough to stay the course?

In summing up this study, here are ten myths we need to firmly reject:

Myth No. One – That man is the center and master of the earth, which gives him the authority to use and abuse it.

Myth No. Two – The Bible has little or nothing to say to us about our relationship to creation since that is the arena of science.

A spiritual and scientific issue. 59

Myth No. Three – Since Heaven is to be our final home we need not worry about saving the earth.

Myth No. Four – Humankind stands above nature and therefore need not share in its suffering.

Myth No. Five – The animals, birds and trees are really our brothers and sisters.

Myth No. Six – The earth will always heal itself.

Myth No. Seven – Humankind has the power to destroy the earth.

Myth No. Eight – This earth will never cease to exist.

Myth No. Nine – New technology will solve GW/CC.

Myth No. Ten – Global warming is primarily a scientific issue, so religion should bug out!

In contrast, here are ten truths we should embrace now:

Truth No. One – God is the creator and sustainer of this world.

Truth No. Two – God delegated dominion over the earth to Adam and Eve and their descendants, but they have often failed in their responsibilities.

Truth No. Three – This failure has damaged creation, causing it to groan and cry out for relief.

Truth No. Four – Despite our failures, God has continued to love us and calls us to better creation care for our broken planet.

Truth No. Five – Creation has much good in it and will respond to proper love and care.

Truth No. Six – Science alone cannot solve the damage that has been done, but healing is possible through a right relationship with God.

Truth No. Seven – The life and teaching of Jesus honored creation and He demonstrated His authority over it.

Truth No. Eight – Jesus taught that in end times climate change and other catastrophic events would accompany God's judgement upon our rebellious culture.

Truth No. Nine – Jesus promised that He would address the groaning of creation by creating a new heaven and a new earth that would be perfect.

Truth No. Ten – The answer to global warming is for all humankind to turn from their rebellion, selfishness and greed, and commit themselves to be diligent and loving servants of God.

What to do??

As a military officer, I learned never to bring up a problem without also bringing a solution. We have now come to the solution phase. The issue of GW/CC is an urgent and long-standing one. It is complex and multi-dimensional and goes to the very heart of our ethics and morality. In the past, when the earth's population was much less, we could ignore many of our destructive practices. But, when our population and technology began to rapidly increase, our capacity to exploit the earth also increased, causing us to reach a critical point. What are some practical things we can all do now?

1. We can seek a clearer vision of God as creator and the world He has made.
2. We can seek a better understanding of our role as keepers of His world.
3. We should approach this duty as a sacred task.
4. We should avoid, at all costs, damaging the planet in such a way that might be irreversible.
5. We should work to clean up the messes left by those who went before us.
6. We should adopt a simpler lifestyle, so there will be enough resources for us and those who follow.

A spiritual and scientific issue. 61

7. We should work to leave our little corner of creation in better condition than we found it.
8. We can accept the killing of animals for food but killing animals for pleasure or trophies should stir our consciences.
9. We must define what is a reasonable quality of life for us, so we will not be driven by greed.
10. We should urge our families, friends, church, community and governments to support behavior and policies that respect our environment.
11. We must all do our part in reducing the greenhouse gases for which we are responsible.

We must do these things because they are the right thing to do, as responsible servants of God.

But what if our global warming today is simply a prelude to the greater Global Warming that is prophesied to take place in the last days? If we are looking at the beginning of something much more profound, then these words of Jesus from Luke 21:34-36 would apply:

> *But watch yourselves lest your hearts be weighed down with dissipation and drunkenness and cares of this life, and that day come upon you suddenly like a trap. For it will come upon all who dwell on the face of the whole earth. But stay awake at all times, praying that you may have strength to escape these things that are going to take place, and stand before the Son of Man.*

The Press often asks President Trump a question to which they expect a precise answer. When he does not have a full vision of the answer, he simply replies, "We'll see what happens." Actually, this is a very wise answer because we cannot always see what is developing before us. The answer "we'll see what happens" might very well apply to GW/CC today. Whatever develops, Christ is urging us to not be discouraged but to watch and wait and work and pray. Isaiah the prophet reminds us in Chapter sixty-five of his book, that God is present and calling to us long before we are ready to hear:

> *I was ready to be sought by those who did not ask for me.... I was ready to be found by those who did not seek me.... I said, "Here I am, here I am." I spread out my hands all day to the rebellious people.... These are a smoke in my nostrils, a fire that burns all the day.*

Could it be that our global warming today is actually a metaphor for our spiritual condition toward God? Could it also be that the sweet incense of our lives which God longs to enjoy has turned into choking smoke in His nostrils because of our rebellion? This again is why we state emphatically that GW/CC is first and foremost a spiritual issue to be acknowledged and dealt with in the heart of humankind.

So, where do we begin? We can begin by offering an honest and humble prayer to our Creator. Here are some words we might consider:

The Lord's Prayer:

> *Our Father which art in Heaven, hallowed be thy name; Thy kingdom come, thy will be done on earth as it is in heaven. Give us this day our daily bread. And forgive us our debts as we forgive our debtors. And lead us not into temptation but deliver us from evil. For thine is the kingdom, and the power, and the glory forever Amen* (Matthew 6:9-13 KJV).

St. Basil's Prayer (from the 4th Century):

> *O God, enlarge within us a sense of fellowship with all living things. . . to whom you give the earth as their home in common with us. We remember with shame that in the past we have exercised the high dominion of man with ruthless cruelty, so that the voice of the earth which should have gone up to you in song, has been a groan of travail. May we realize that they live not for us alone but for themselves and for thee, and that they love the sweetness of life.* (Passion for the Earth, p. 164)

A spiritual and scientific issue.

A prayerful hymn:

This is my Father's world, O let me ne'er forget
That though the wrong seems oft so strong,
God is the Ruler yet.
This is my Father's world, the battle is not done;
Jesus who died shall be satisfied,
And earth and heav'n be one.
by Maltbie D. Babcock

Let us determine to exercise our dominion over the Earth in the spirit of Christ, of whom it was said, *"He came not to be served but to serve."* (Mark 10:45)

SELECTED BIBLIOGRAPHY

Barnes-Davis, Rebecca J. *50 Ways to Help Save the Earth*. Louisville, KY: Westminster John Knox Press, 2009.

Bastardi, Joe. *The Climate Chronicles: What Al Gore Did Not Tell You – and Others*. Minneapolis: Relentless Thunder Press, 2018.

Berry, Wendell. *The Gift of Good Land*. Berkley, CA: Counterpoint Press, 1981.

Collins, Paul. *Judgement Day*. Maryknoll, NY: Orbis Books, 2011.

Coleson, Joseph, Ed. *Care of Creation: Voice's on God, Humanity*. Indianapolis: Wesleyan Publishing, 2011.

Conradie, Ernst. *Saving the Earth? The Legacy of Reformed Views on "re-creation"*. Hamburg, Germany: Lit Verlag, 2013.

Conroy, Donald and Rodney Peterson. *Earth At Risk*. Amhurst, NY: Humanity Books, 2000.

Edwards, Dennis. *Ecology At the Heart of Faith*. Maryknoll, NY: Orbis Books, 2006.

Flannery, Tim. *Weather Makers*. New York: Grove Press, 2006.

Fowler, Robert. *The Greening of Protestant Thought*. Chapel Hill: University of North Carolina Press, 1995.

Gilkey, Langdon. *Maker of Heaven and Earth*. Garden City, NY: Doubleday and Co., 1959.

Goodell, Jeff. *The Water Will Come*. New York: Little, Brown Co., 2017.

Gore, Al. *An Inconvenient Truth*. London: Penguin Book Ltd., 2008.

Habel, Norma and Vicky Balabanski, Eds. *The Earth Story in the New Testament*. Cleveland: Pilgrim Press, 2002.

Hansen, James. *Storms of My Grandchildren*. New York: Bloomsbury Press, 2009.

Hayhoe, Katherine and Andrew Fraley. *A Climate For Change*. New York: Faith Words Hachette Book Group, 2016.

Larson, Dale and Sandy. *While Creation Waits*. Wheaton: Harold Shaw Publishers, 1992.

LeQuire, Stan, Ed. *The Best Preaching On Earth*. Valley Forge: Judson Press, 1996.

McDonagh, Sean. *Passion For The Earth*. Maryknoll, NY: Orbis Books, 1994.

Merritt, Jonathan. *Green Like God*. New York: Faith Words Hachette Book Group, 2010.

Michaelson, Wesley G. *Ecology and Life*. Waco: Word Books, 1988.

Moo, Jonathan and Robert White. *Let Creation Rejoice*. Downers Grove, IL: Varsity Press, 2014.

Nash, James A. *Loving Nature*. Nashville: Abingdon Press, 1991.

Northcott, Michael S. *A Political Theology of Climate Change*. Grand Rapids: Wm. B. Eerdmans Publishing Co., 2013.

Rogers, Elizabeth and Thomas Kostigen. *The Green Book*. New York: Three Rivers Press, 2007.

Sabin, Scott C. *Tending to Eden*. Valley Forge: Judson Press, 2010.

Scranton, Roy. *Living to Die in Anthropocene – Reflections on the End of Civilization*. San Francisco: City Lights Publishers, 2015.

Snyder, Howard. *Salvation Means Creation Healed*. Eugene, OR: Cascade Books, 2011

Van Dyke, Fred. *Between Heaven and Earth*. Santa Barbara: Praeger, 2010.

Wallace, Mark. *Green Christianity*. Minneapolis: Fortress Press, 2010.

Wilson, Jonathan R. *God's Good World*. Grand Rapids: Baker Publishing Co.

About the Author

After a long career of 33 years serving with the Navy, Marine Corps and Coast Guard, Chaplain Cook retired as Command Chaplain, Pearl Harbor Naval Base. Following retirement from the Navy, he took time out to finish a Doctor of Ministry Degree at Asbury Theological Seminary on the subject of transition from the civilian pastorate into the military chaplaincy. Upon completion of the degree, he taught in the Religion Department of Roberts Wesleyan College in Rochester, NY, where he also created and served in their first position of college chaplain. In addition, he accepted the position of the Director of Free Methodist Chaplains, serving in this capacity for several years.

After teaching at Roberts Wesleyan, he was appointed as senior pastor of the Wilmore Free Methodist Church in Wilmore, KY, where he also served as director of the denomination's students at Asbury Theological Seminary as well as adjunct professor at the Seminary.

Upon retirement in 2004, he devoted himself to writing. In addition to *Global Warming and End-Times: A Spiritual and Scientific Issue,* Dean has also written:
- **Salt of the Sea**: *A Navy Chaplain's Experience Ashore and at Sea*
  November 2005, ISBN 978-1597817127
- **Chaplaincy**: *Being God's Presence in Closed Communities*
  March 2010, ISBN 978-1449083014
- **Jonah**: *The Man Whose God and Heart Were Too Small*
  January 2015, ISBN 978-1496962867
- **Where Have All the Prophets Gone?**
  October 2017, ISBN 978-1545616055

All of Dr. E. Dean Cook's works can be obtained by ordering at your local bookstore, or online at Amazon.com or other online book retailers.

In addition to writing, he has continued to teach and preach and speak at camps, conferences and retreats. He has also served on the Central Kentucky Veterans Committee and assisted candidates seeking ordination and/or entrance into the chaplaincy.

www.ingramcontent.com/pod-product-compliance
Lightning Source LLC
Chambersburg PA
CBHW020021050426
42450CB00005B/583